DOONESBURY BOOKS BY G.B. TRUDEAU

Still a Few Bugs in the System
The President Is a Lot Smarter Than You Think
But This War Had Such Promise
Call Me When You Find America
Guilty, Guilty, Guilty!
"What Do We Have for the Witnesses, Johnnie?"
Dare To Be Great, Ms. Caucus
Wouldn't a Gremlin Have Been More Sensible?
"Speaking of Inalienable Rights, Amy..."
You're Never Too Old for Nuts and Berries
An Especially Tricky People
As the Kid Goes for Broke
Stalking the Perfect Tan
"Any Grooming Hints for Your Fans, Rollie?"
But the Pension Fund Was Just Sitting There
We're Not Out of the Woods Yet
A Tad Overweight, but Violet Eyes to Die For
And That's My Final Offer!
He's Never Heard of You, Either
In Search of Reagan's Brain
Ask for May, Settle for June
Unfortunately, She Was Also Wired for Sound
The Wreck of the "Rusty Nail"
You Give Great Meeting, Sid
Doonesbury: A Musical Comedy
Check Your Egos at the Door
That's *Doctor* Sinatra, You Little Bimbo!
Death of a Party Animal
Downtown Doonesbury
Calling Dr. Whoopee

IN LARGE FORMAT

The Doonesbury Chronicles
Doonesbury's Greatest Hits
The People's Doonesbury
Doonesbury Dossier: The Reagan Years
Doonesbury Deluxe: Selected Glances Askance

# Doonesbury's GREATEST HITS

## G. B. Trudeau

An Owl Book
Henry Holt and Company
New York

Published by Henry Holt and Company, Inc.,
115 West 18th Street, New York, New York 10011.
Published in Canada by Fitzhenry & Whiteside Limited,
195 Allstate Parkway, Markham, Ontario L3R 4T8.

Library of Congress Catalog Card Number: 78-53780
ISBN Hardbound: 0-03-044851-4
ISBN Paperback: 0-8050-0883-7

Designer: Libra Graphics, Inc.
Printed in the United States of America

The cartoons in this book have appeared in newspapers
in the United States and abroad under the auspices of
Universal Press Syndicate.

10   9   8

ISBN 0-03-044851-4 HARDBOUND
ISBN 0-8050-0883-7 PAPERBACK

"If that's art, then I'm a Hottentot."

—*Harry S. Truman*

# Overture

It was graduation day at Yale and I flicked through the official program to the page that would give the names of the people fetching honorary degrees. Subconsciously one looks for a Surprise. Marshal Ky would have qualified in 1976. I noticed the name of Trudeau, and uttered a silent prayer of gratitude for Yale's tradition against speeches by endoctored celebrities. It turned out of course to be another Trudeau, one of whom I had not heard; only a year or two older than my graduating son. I assumed he was a local divinity of sorts, indeed he was so treated—I think I remember rightly that only he received a standing ovation from the graduating class when his name was called out. Perhaps he had invented the neutron bomb? I remembered somebody telling me that all geniuses in the physical sciences discover their fourth dimensions when they are twenty-two years old. My surprise was genuine, upon hearing the citation, to deduce that he was an artist, or social critic; indeed he was festooned so lavishly by the president of Yale that I wondered how it could be that I had not heard his name before. On mentioning this later to my astonished son I was made to feel as though I had not heard of an entire world war. I strained to see, but from mid-crowd everyone wearing reading glasses and an academic gown looks pretty much the same—and anyway, what did it matter? I did not suppose that merely *looking* at G.B. Trudeau would make me laugh, the way merely looking at Jack Benny used to make me laugh. I have dug up the citation read out at New Haven that springy afternoon, and search it out now for the hyperbole that usually breaks one's back in the rhetoric of honorary degrees. Listen . . .

"Yale's image, as the hucksters would say, would never be the same after what you have done to your classmates and your President. Happily, too, your country will never look at itself quite as self-seriously, certainly not as self-righteously, thanks to your satiric insights into the foibles and pretensions of both the notorious and the obscure. For helping keep us sane even when the times seem crazed, Yale, with pride and delight, confers upon her recent son the degree of Doctor of Humane Letters."

I made a note to look out for what I was informed went out to the newspapers of the world six times a week under the rubric *Doonesbury.* But since I tend to read only *The New York Times,* my resolution flagged; and it was not until receiving this invitation to review his work that I undertook the assignment industriously. I think it is in one way unfair to Mr. Trudeau to have done this to him. Last year a mad musician performed all thirty-two sonatas of Ludwig van Beethoven without interruption, and I cannot imagine anyone doing this as a true act of homage. Yet during the past two weeks every time I have traveled it has been with a briefcase crammed full of *Doonesbury.* People of all ages have certainly thought me reverted to infantilism as they see the comic strips spread about me. But those who looked me in the eye would have detected that I share Yale's pride and delight.

What is there to say about *Doonesbury*, or even about the comic-strip mode? Never having studied a strip before, it is conceivable that I notice things that are generally unnoticed by those continuingly familiar with the genre, even as I notice the loud noise at rock concerts. There is, for instance, the nagging mechanical—and therefore artistic—problem of reintroducing the reader to the synoptic point at which he was dropped the day before. In a collection this is more aggravating than if twenty-four hours have gone by since arriving at the point where the artist left you, and you need a little nudge. Trudeau handles this very deftly, usually by introducing into the panel a tilt of some sort that takes the reader slightly beyond where he was left yesterday, so that he is relieved of that awful sensation of turning wheels without moving forward.

The other problem is the presumptive requirement of the climax—the gag—at the end of every strip. This cadence no artist can hope to satisfy, although they must all make the effort. A collection runs the risk of maximizing the disharmonies. Imagine reading a collection of the last paragraphs of Art Buchwald's columns. Or, as Zonker would put it, Imagine! Which digression brings me to note the awful overuse of the intensifier in Mr. Trudeau's captions. Nothing appears so workaday as to be merely remarkable. Everything is *arresting*! Now this is in sharp stylistic contrast with the very nearly expressionless faces Mr. Trudeau tends to draw. Nobody ever smiles, or hardly ever; and the effect is wonderful, insofar as it reminds the reader that no experience, no absurdity, no observation, is truly new. But nearly everything spoken must be punctuated with exclamation points and served up in boldface type. I am as unconvinced that this is necessary as I am persuaded that Trudeau scores remarkably well in wrenching a climax of sorts out of almost every one of his strips. There are the anticlimaxes; but the reader forgives them indulgently; he is well enough nourished, all the more so since there is all that wonderful assonant humor and derision in mid-panel: indeed, not infrequently the true climaxes come in the penultimate panel, and the rest is lagniappe.

And then—there is a sense of rhetorical leisure in Trudeau. *Whatever* is the *hurry*? It is very pleasurable, the more so when one realizes how compressive the form is by nature, like smoking a cigar on a parachute jump. After reading three years' worth of *Doonesbury* I am certain I have read as many words as are in *War and Peace*. The artist gives off a great air of authority by this device, rather like those notices in *The New Yorker* magazine in which even the most conventional abbreviations are spurned ("Closed on Sundays and holidays, except for Thanksgiving").

Consider the treatment of an essentially banal exchange. If it were honed less finely, it would not work. One of the characters is watching a television screen, whence the words sound out:

"At the very root of the Big Apple's problems seems to be the endless exodus of the middle class. 'Good Night, New York' is fortunate to have with us tonight Mr. Jamie Dodd, one such fugitive.

"Jamie, I take it you and your wife have always been anxious to leave New York? . . ."

"Oh no, not at all, Geraldo—in fact, at first the city seemed a marvelous place for an upwardly mobile couple like us! [Note the exclamation point.] But then one day last fall I was promoted to a $45,000 job. That same day my wife was assaulted in the park. The power went off, and the garbage people went on strike . . . And suddenly! Right! Suddenly Darien made *loads* of sense!"

It requires a hypnotic self-assurance to bring off (as Trudeau does) that sequence. As so often, he relies heavily on his meiotic pen to do it.

The longueurs are sometimes almost teasingly didactic. Who else in the funny-paper business would attempt the following?

[Again, the action is coming out of the television set.]

"Mr. Finkles, as one of New York's past comptrollers, how were you able to build up such a whopping deficit?"

"Well Geraldo, we had *many* great tricks. The most common one was selling city bonds on the strength of inflated estimates of anticipated federal funding. This device was very popular among top city money wizards. But let me show you my personal favorite. See Column B here? This is where we charged the final wage period of one fiscal year to the budget of the next! In so doing, we built up a hidden deficit of *two billion dollars*!"

"Wow!"

"Now I must caution the folks at home from trying this . . ."

Note the touch of the anticlimax in the last line, inserted in the way that Oliphant permits the kitten or the mouse to pronounce the moral coda. But the unapologetically literate account of the exact character of the financial hanky-panky gives a rollicking sense of reality to the episode.

Note also: "Geraldo." Trudeau likes to identify his characters, and he is quite willing to be personal.

"Good morning. [We see a telephone receptionist.] *New York Daily News* promotion department."

"Yes, hello. I'm about to kill someone and I'd like to talk to somebody about coverage."

"Yes sir. Would this be an isolated crime of passion, or will you be making a habit of it?"

"Uh, I don't know . . . I'm not sure . . . I mean I don't know my long-range plans yet . . ."

"I'm sorry, sir, but we have to know what sort of story yours is."

"Mine is a story of hopelessness and shattered dreams in the city they call New York."

"Fine. That would be Mr. Breslin. Please hold."

Duke, recalled as ambassador from China, is trying to go back to free-lance journalism, but he is in despair. "Wenner won't even return my calls, so I guess a job at *Rolling Stone* is out."

"Amazing. After all you've been through you'd think he'd at least lend a hand."

"Nope. He needs them both for social climbing."

Duke, by the way, is relieved as chargé in China by Leonard Woodcock. "Leonard Woodcock! I just can't get over it! Whatever could have possessed Carter to pick Woodcock for China?"

"Well, sir [says his Chinese interpreter], maybe it's because Mr. Woodcock's career has been one of great sensitivity to the plight of the working class!"

"Honey, all labor leaders are sensitive to the working class. That's how they avoid belonging to it."

The willingness to criticize the union bureaucracy reminds us with relief that Trudeau, who sprang from the loins of the Vietnam antinomianism, quickly achieved perspective. There is the radio phone-in talk show. The host is talking:

"Was our squalid, cynical mission in Vietnam ever really worth the price? Was it ever worth the . . ."

RING! RING!

"Hello, this is a listener, and I'm sick of your autopsy! Get off it and stop dwelling in the past! It's *over*, hear me?—It's over!"

"Lissen, buddy, the Vietnam debacle rightly occasions a reassessment of our national purposes. We're doin' this gig for the future. We're doin' it for your children!"

"My children? They're in bed."

Indeed, let the coopters beware (remember Al Capp?). G.B. Trudeau isn't thirty yet, and listen to this indoctrination class in Saigon now that the FLN have taken over.

"Yes?" [The teacher is responding to a question from a trainee.]

"Excuse me, sir, but I don't think I belong in this class. I already know most of this stuff."

"What's your name? I'll check the printout."

"Tho. I'm a former commissioned officer."

"Tho? Lou Tho, Jr.? You were assigned to this class?"

"Yup."

"That's funny—you were meant to be shot."

"No, that's Dad—Lou, Sr."

Those in search of the meaning of humane letters need go no further than to *Doonesbury*.

WILLIAM F. BUCKLEY, JR.

# ACT ONE

### Time: 1975 (Early Post-Watergate)

## Selected Scenes

"Tales from the Margaret Mead Taproom" . . . . . Duke, Zonker
"Little Orphan Kimmy" . . . . . . . . . . . . . . . . . . . . The Rosenthals
"Last Plane from Saigon" . . . . . . . . . . . . . . . . . . . . . Phred, B.D.
Bicentennial Interlude: "The Birth of a Nation"
   (Nate's version) . . . . . . . . . . . . . . . . . . . . . . . . . . The Harrises,
                                                                            Minutemen
"Operation Frequent Manhood"
   (Dance Macabre) . . . . . . . . . . . . . . . . . . . . . . Duke, MacArthur,
                                                                            U.S. Marines
"Courts and Torts" . . . . . . . . . . . . . . . . . . . . . . . Joanie, Ginny,
                                                                            Woody
"You're Never Too Old for Nuts and Berries" . . Zonker, Mike,
                                                                            Mr. Harris
Bicentennial Interlude: "The Birth of a Nation"
   (Amy's version) . . . . . . . . . . . . . . . . . . . . . . . . . The Harrises,
                                                                            Paul Revere
"I'm Gay, I'm Cheerful" . . . . . . . . . . . . . . . . . . . . . Andy, Joanie

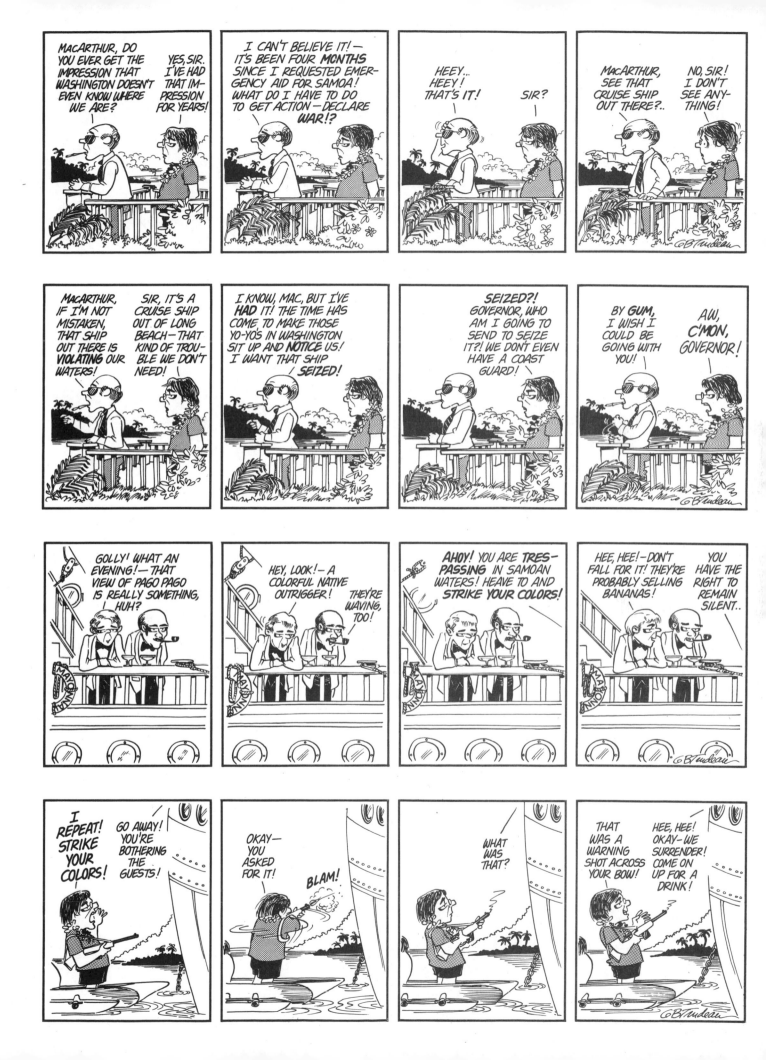

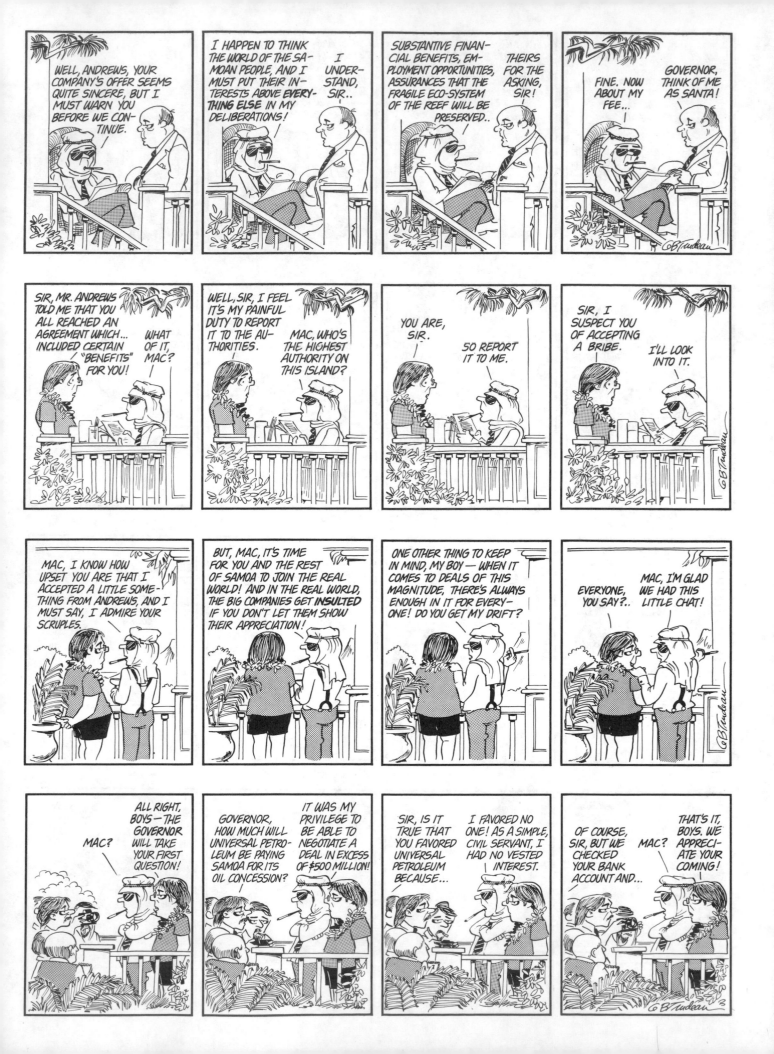

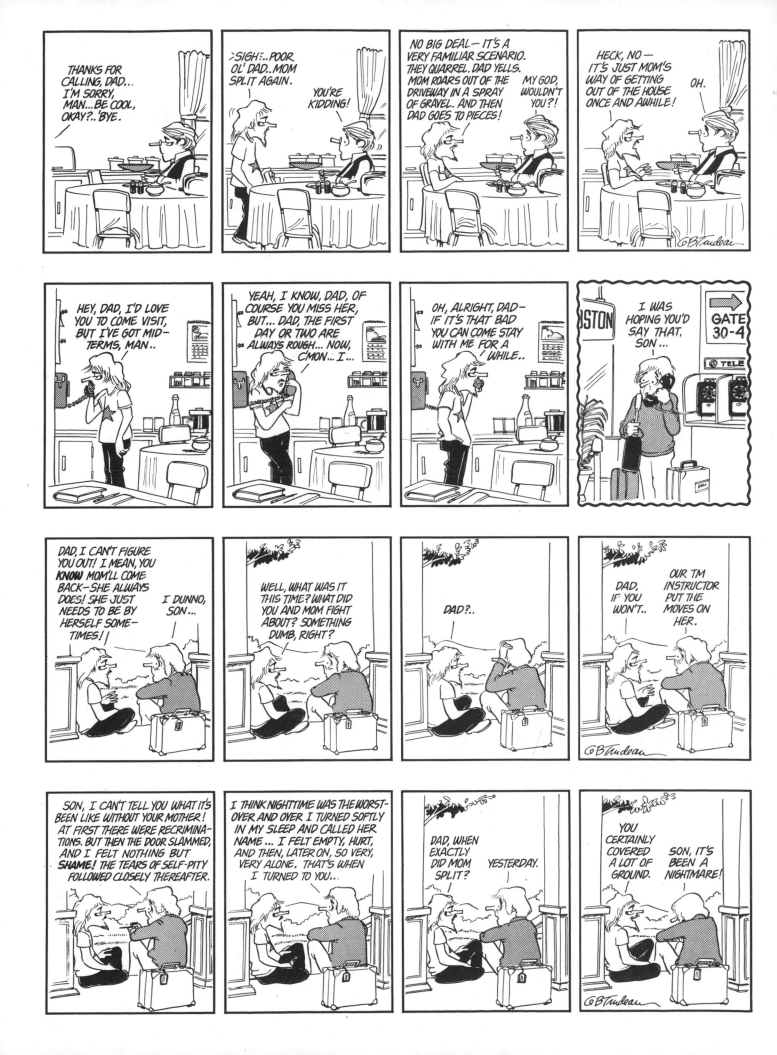

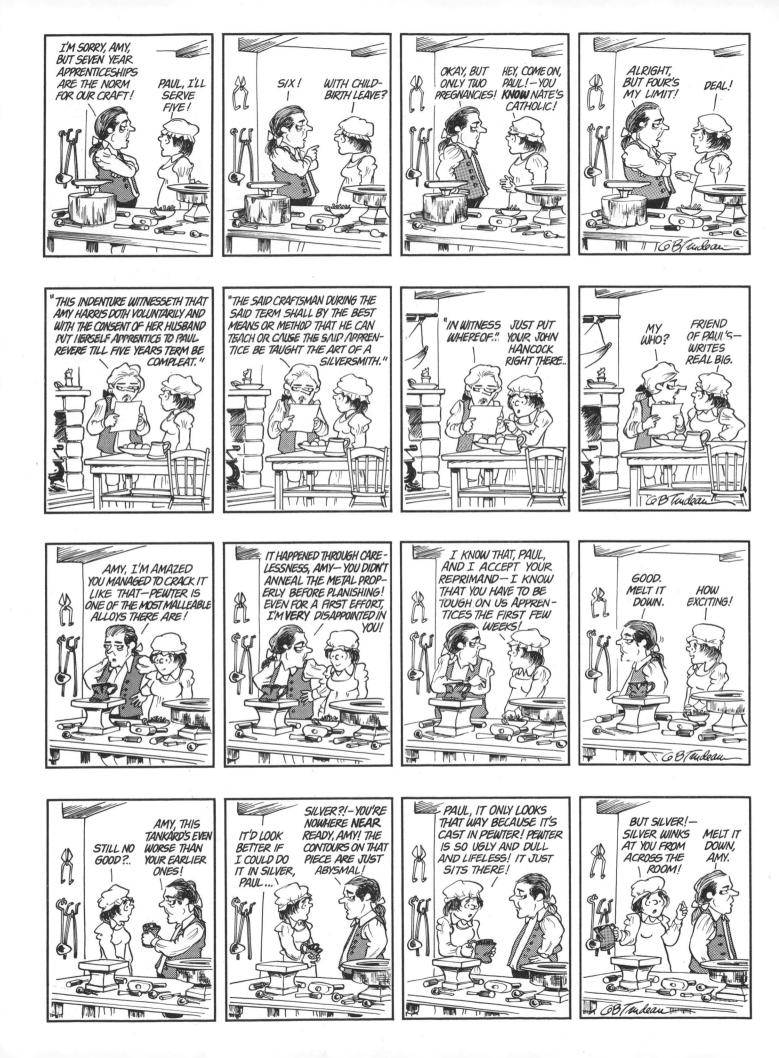

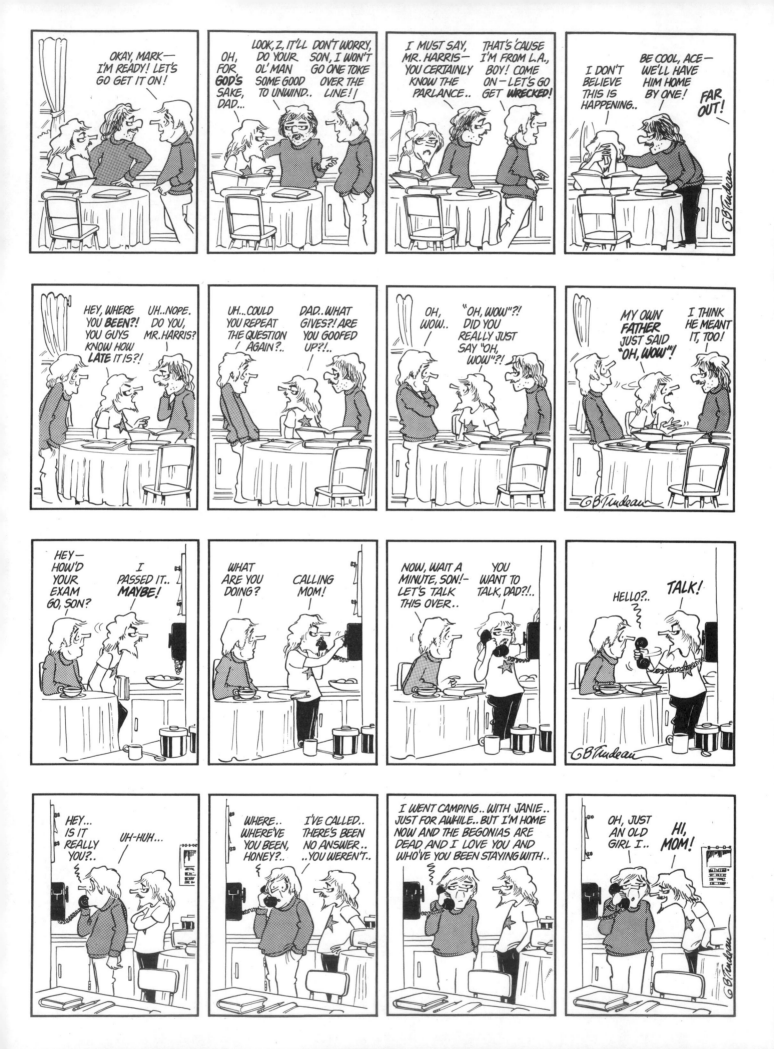

# ACT TWO

*Time: 1976 (The Year of the Dragon)*

*Selected Scenes*

''An Especially Tricky People'' . . . . . . . . . . . . . . . Duke, Chinese
dignitaries
''Ginny's Song'' (pop version) . . . . . . . . . . . Jimmy Thudpucker
''Going the Contrition Route'' . . . . . . . . . . . . The Watergators,
Scott Meredith
''Ginny's Song'' (disco version) . . . . . . . . Jimmy Thudpucker,
Walden West
Rhythm Section
''The Rains in Plains'' . . . . . . . . . . . . . . . . . Jimmy Carter, Jerry
Ford, reporters
''Bluestockings Blues'' . . . . . . . . . . . . . . . . . . . . . Ginny, Lacey
''As the Kid Goes for Broke'' . . . . . . . . . . . . . . . . . Joanie, Rick
''Everybody Does It'' . . . . . . . . . . . . . . . . . . . Senator Ventura,
Miss Tibbet,
Dan Rather
''The Walls Tell All'' . . . . . . . . . . . . . . . . . . . . . . . . . Duke, Honey

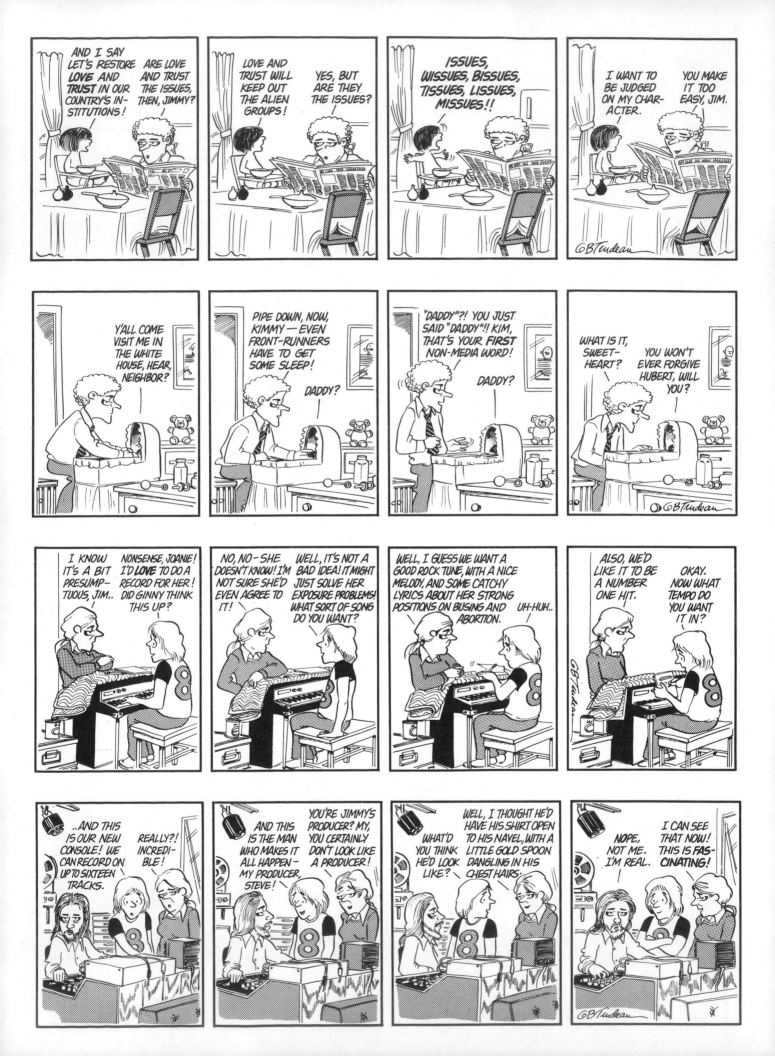

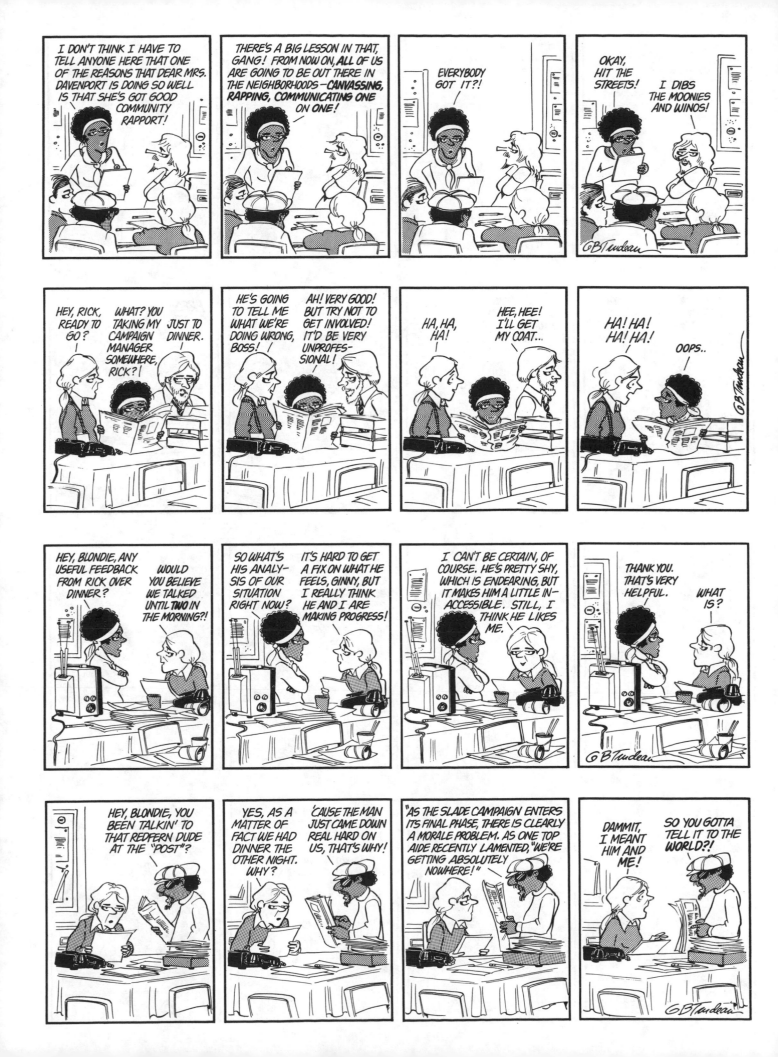

# ACT THREE

*Time: 1977 (Early Disco)*

*Selected Scenes:*

"People Who Hype People" . . . . . . . . . . . . . . . . . . Rick, Brenda
"The Braxton-Hicks Backbeat" . . . . . . . . . . . . . . Jimmy, Jenny,
Feedback
"Something From Gandhi" . . . . . . . . . . . . . . Duane Delacourt
"Ta Da!" (Mortarboard Reverie) . . . . . . . . . . . . . . . . . Joanie
"Why Woodcock?" (Duke's Lament) . . . . . . . . . . Duke, Honey
"Stalking the Perfect Tan" . . . . . . . . . . . . . . . . Zonker, Cornell
"The Koreagate Rag" . . . . . . . . . . . . . . . . . . . . . . Joanie, Lacey,
U.S. Congress
"Original Panama Follies" . . . . . . . . . . . . . . . . . . . Zonker, B.D.,
Kirby
"Back to You, Barbara" . . . . . . . . . . . . . . . . . . . Roland Burton
Hedley, Jr.,
Marvelous Mark
"Sixties Revival Party" (coda) . . . . . . . . . . . . . . . . . . Ensemble

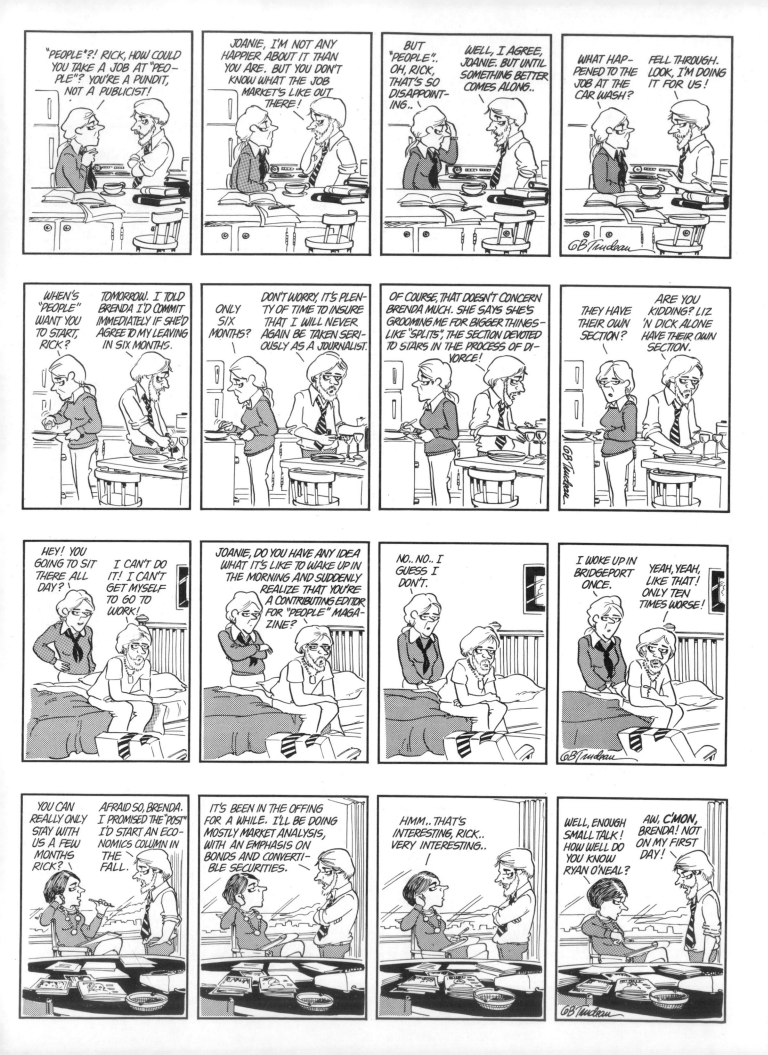

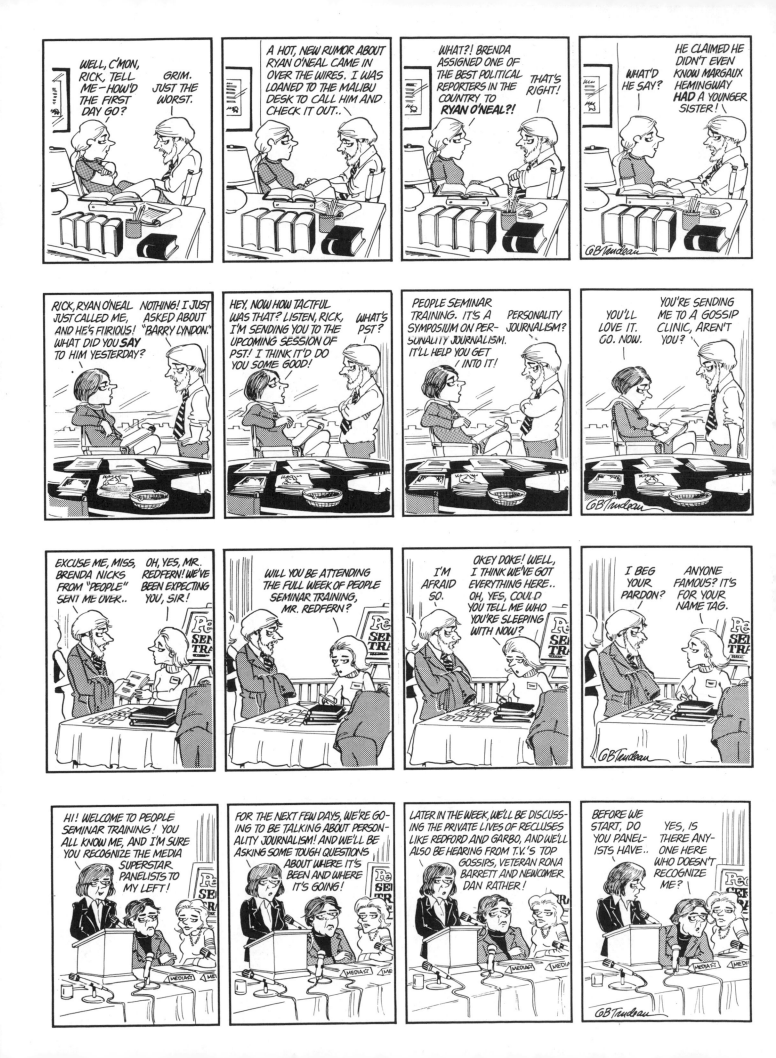

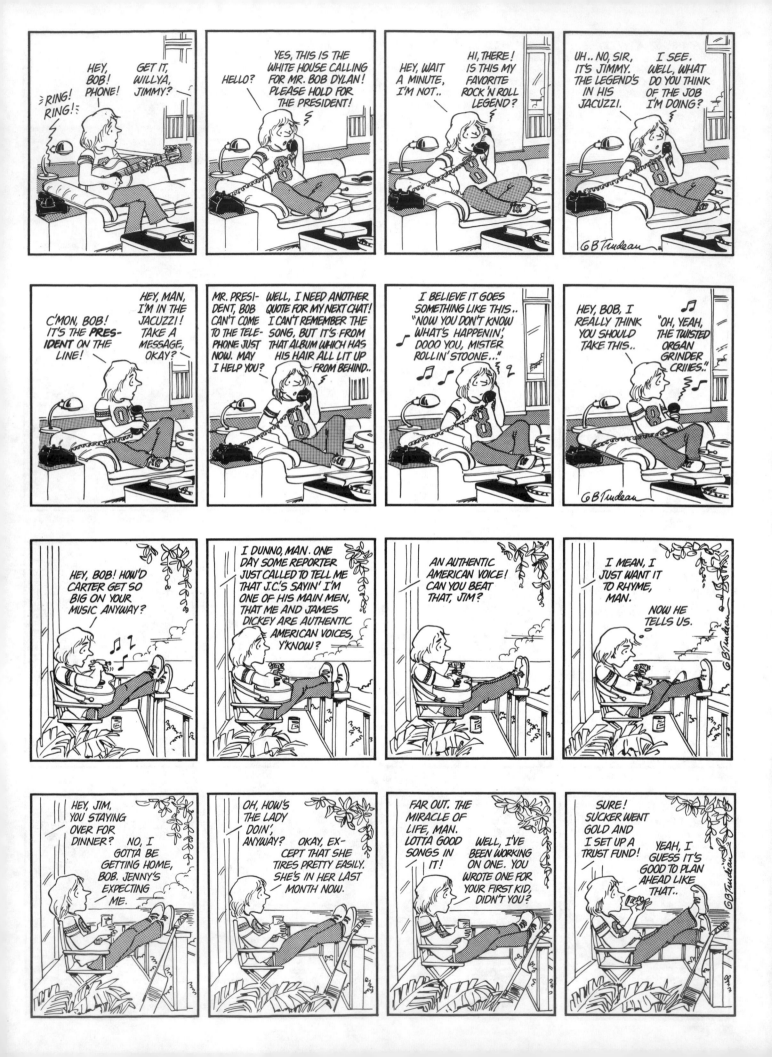

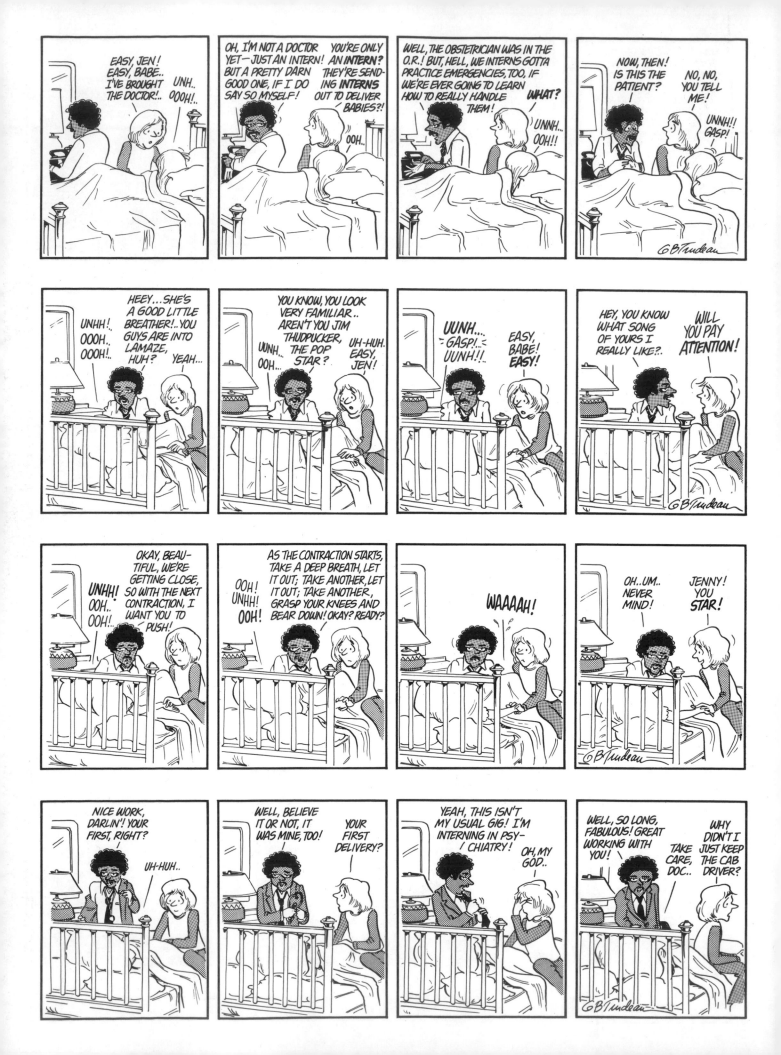

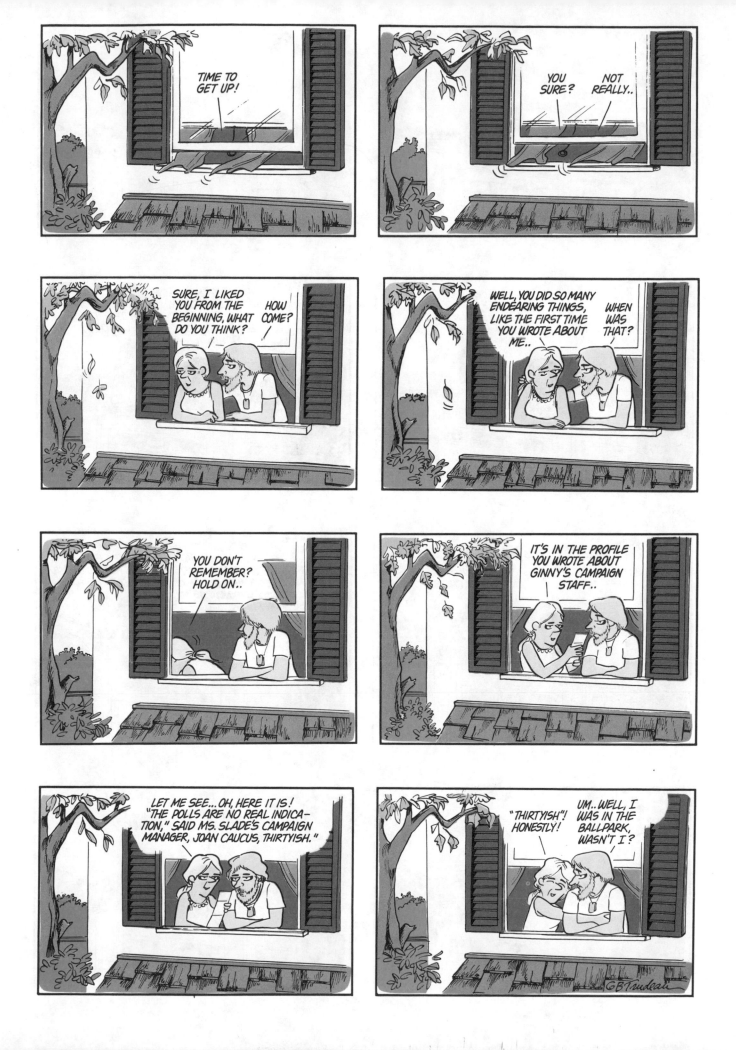

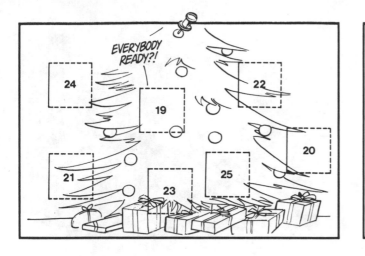

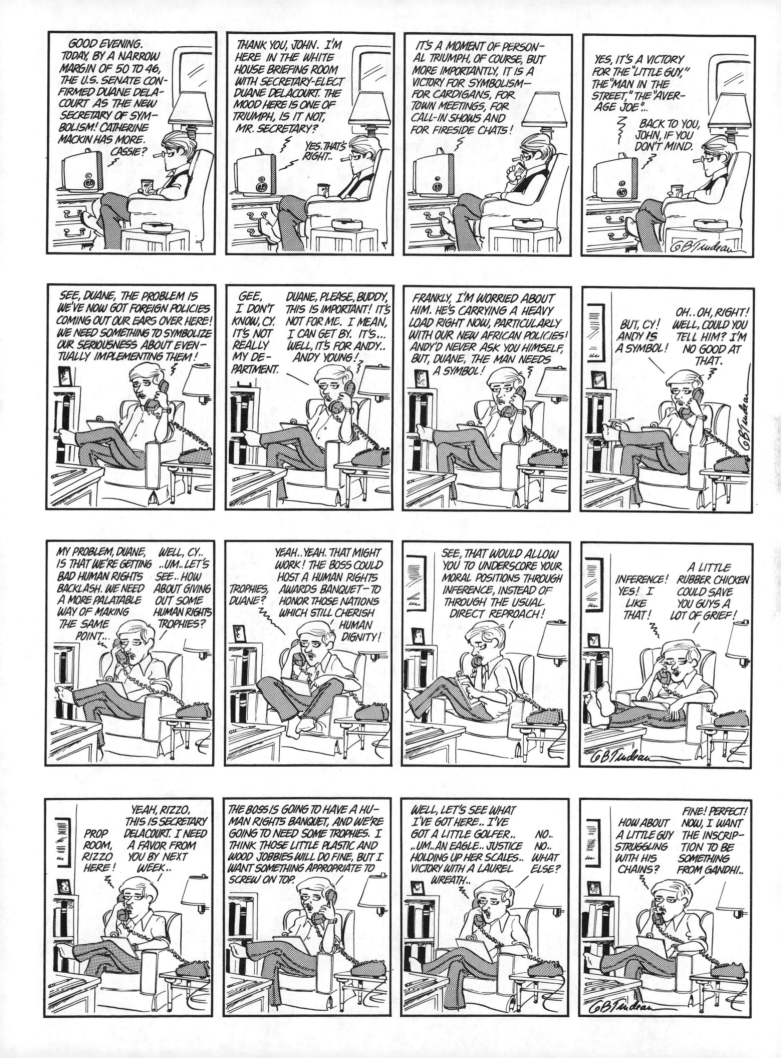

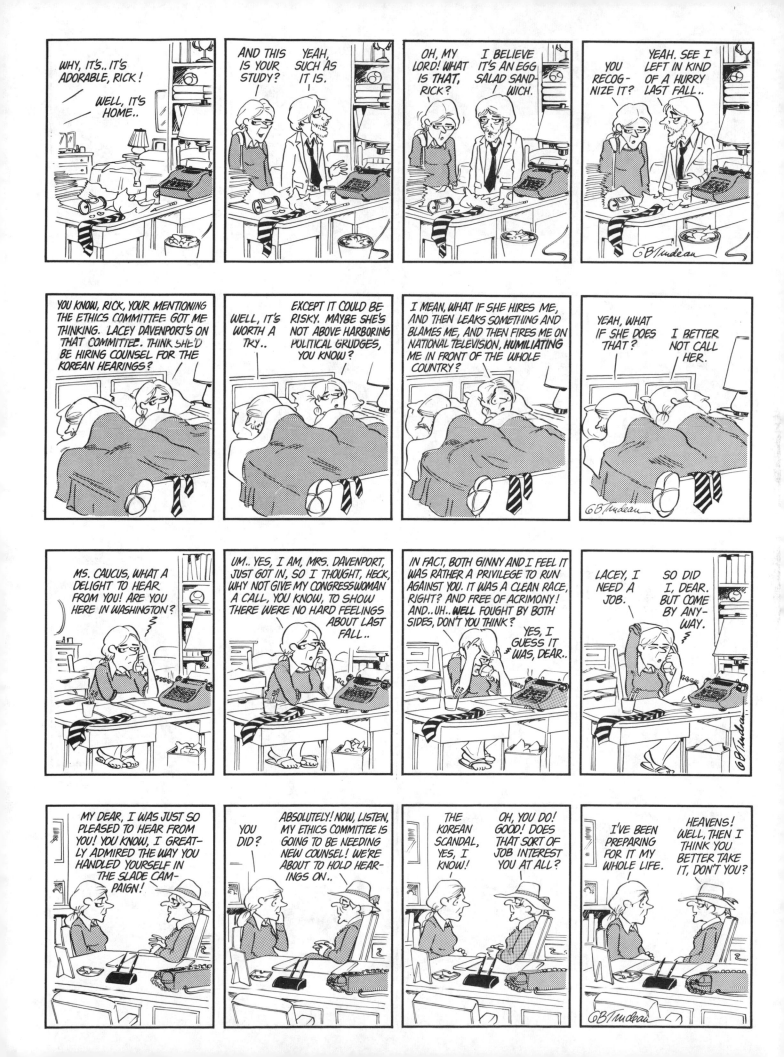

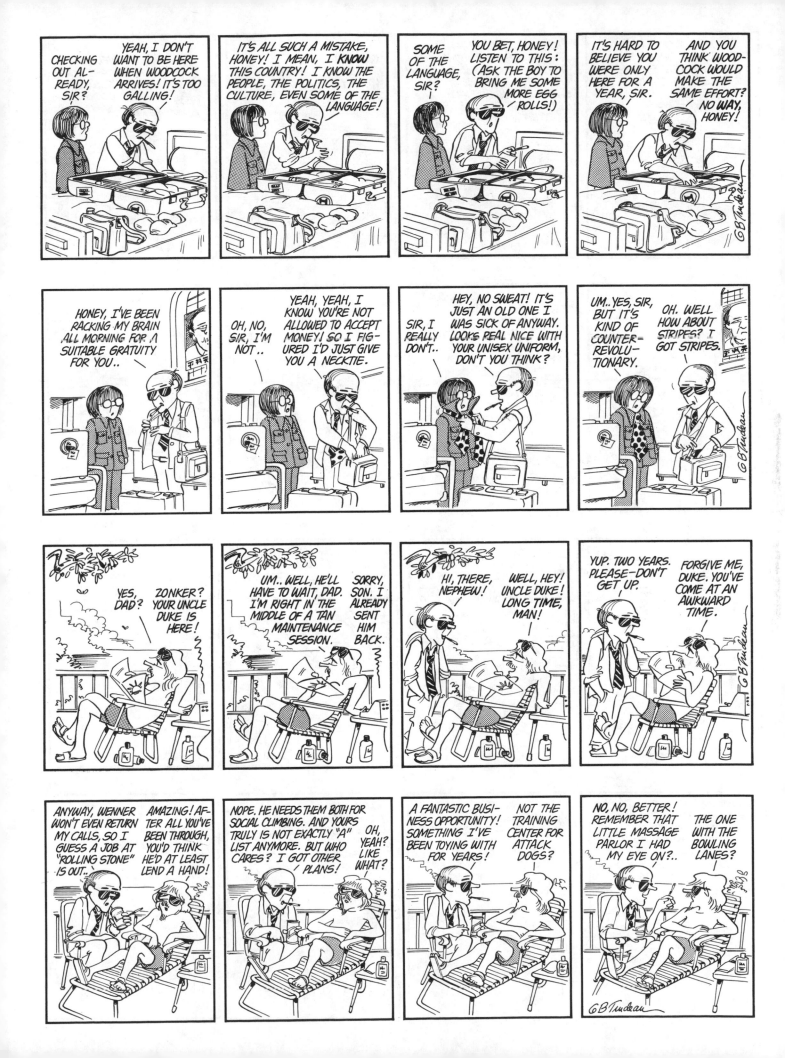

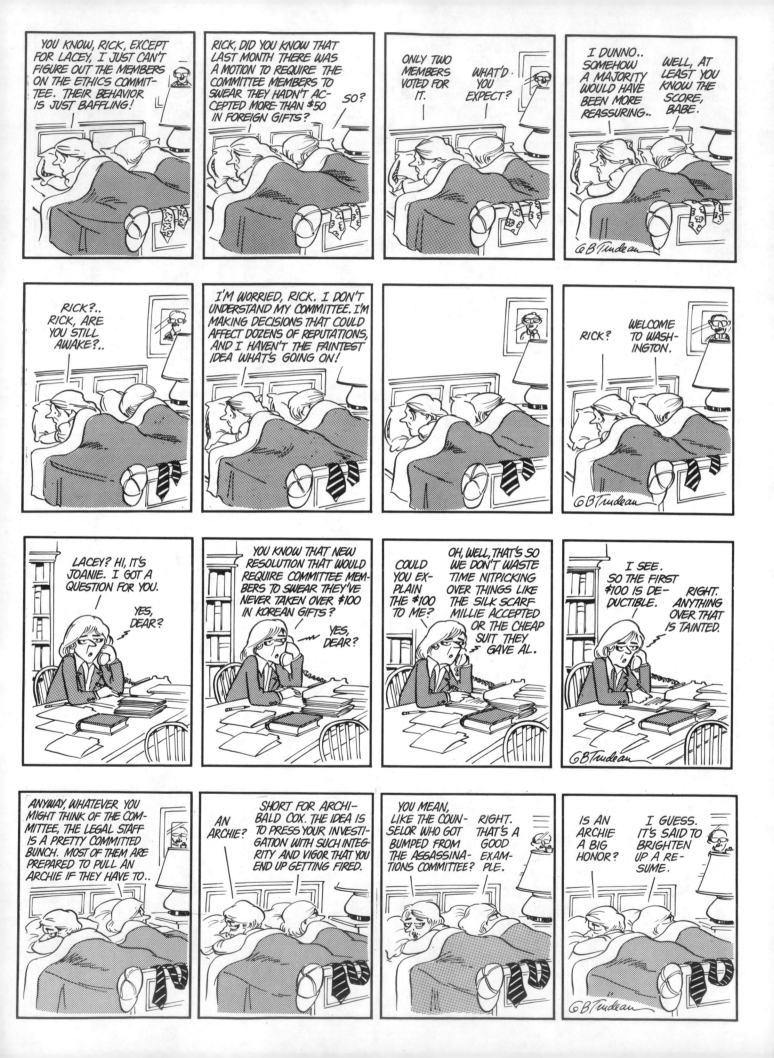

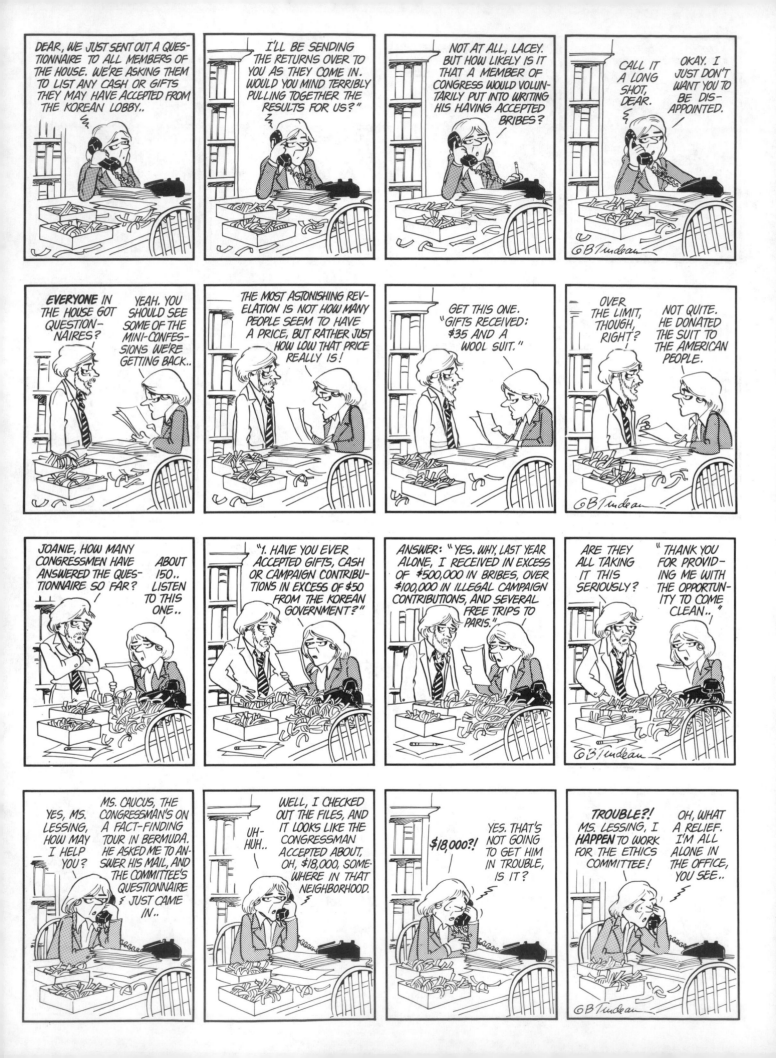

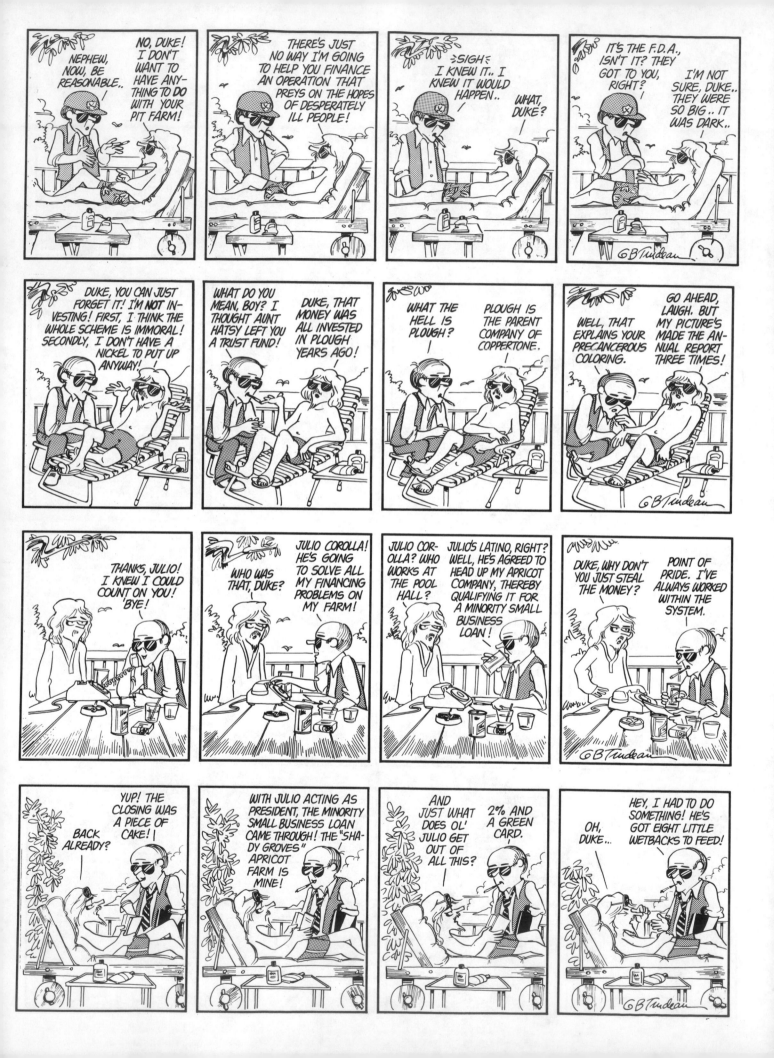

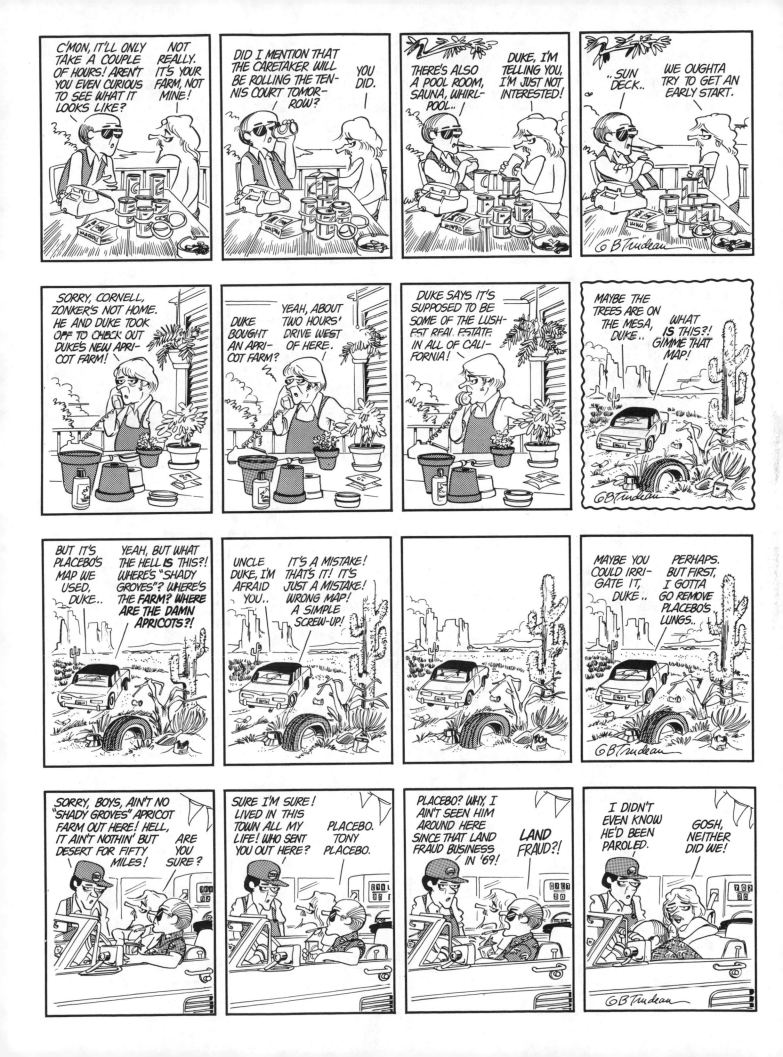

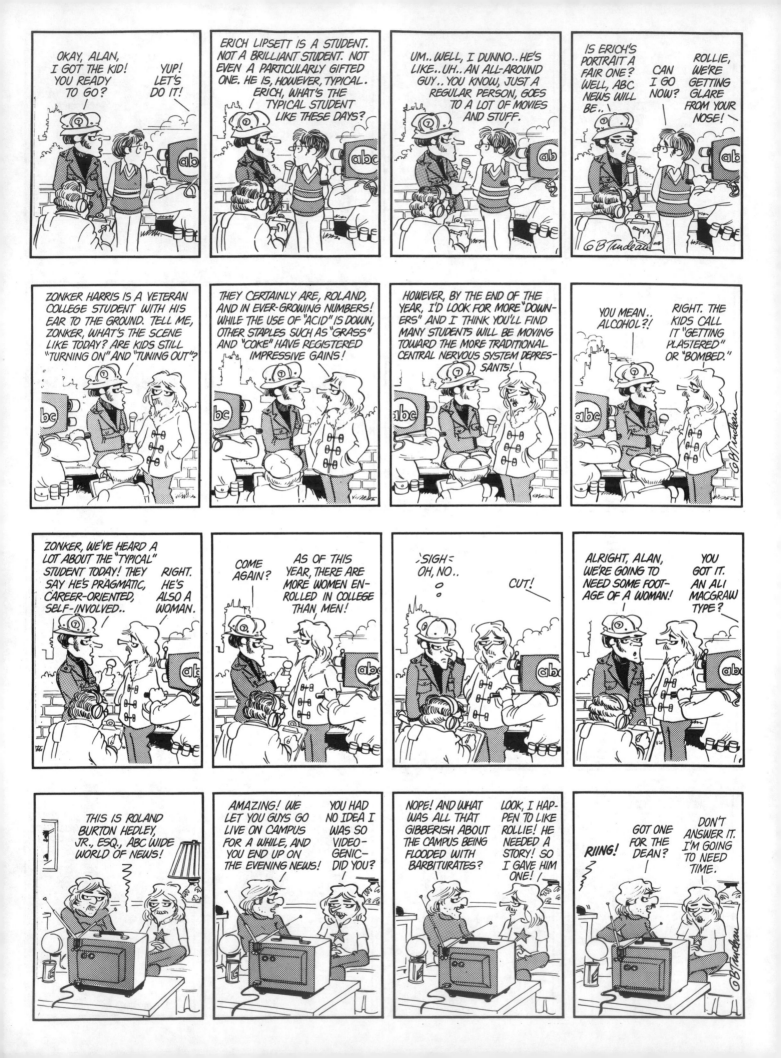

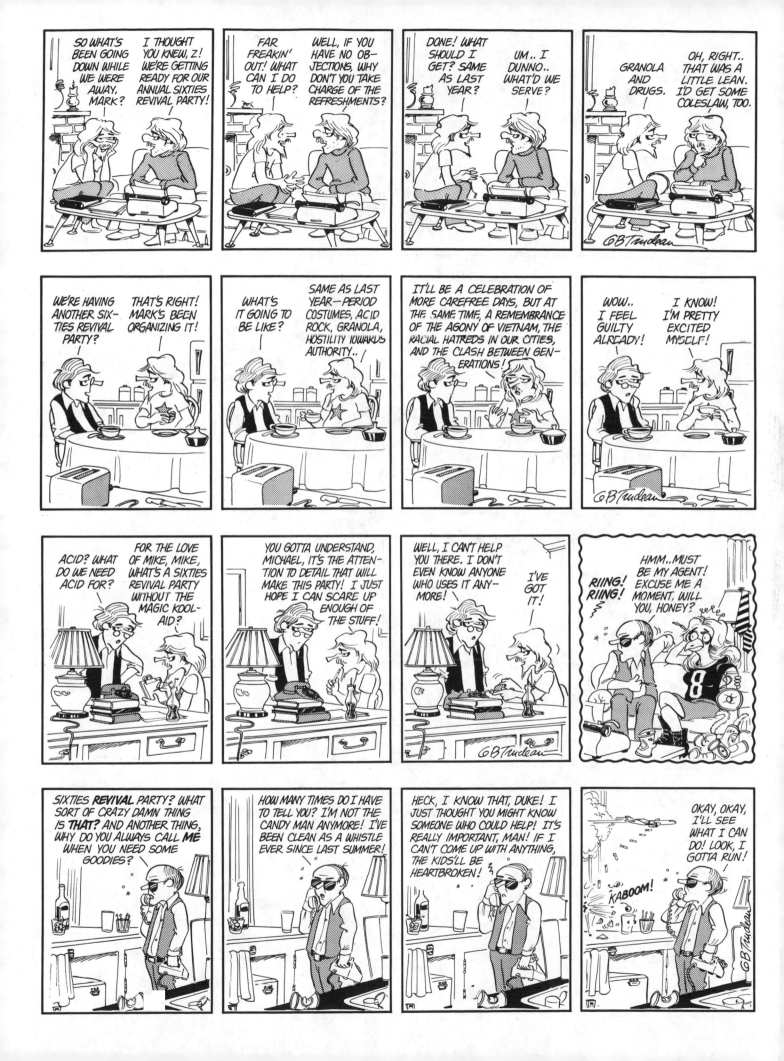